HOW DO THEY HELP? HOW DO THEY HELP? HOW DO THEY HELP?

KIDS SAVING THE RAINFOREST

CHARITIES STARTED BY KIDS!

BY MELISSA SHERMAN PEARL AND DAVID A. SHERMAN

Published in the United States of America by Cherry Lake Publishing
Ann Arbor, Michigan
www.cherrylakepublishing.com

Reading Adviser: Marla Conn MS, Ed., Literacy specialist, Read-Ability, Inc.

Photo Credits: Photos used with permission from Kids Saving the Rainforest, Cover, 1, 11, 13, 15, 17, 19, 21; © Hugh Lansdown / Shutterstock.com, 5; © Pefcon / Shutterstock.com, 7; © Rich Carey / Shutterstock.com, 9

LIBRARY OF CONGRESS CATALOGING-IN-PUBLICATION DATA HAS BEEN FILED AND IS AVAILABLE AT CATALOG.LOC.GOV

Cherry Lake Publishing would like to acknowledge the work of The Partnership for 21st Century Learning. Please visit *www.p21.org* for more information.

Printed in the United States of America
Corporate Graphics

KIDS SAVING THE RAINFOREST

CONTENTS

LIFE IN THE RAINFORESTS

Costa Rica, a small country in Central America, is home to some of the world's most beautiful rainforests. Filled with trees, rainforests are an important part of our environment. Through a process called **photosynthesis**, trees create oxygen for us to breathe. This is why rainforests are often called Earth's lungs.

More than 50 percent of Earth's species live in rainforests. But rainforests only make up 2 percent of Earth's total surface.

LOOK!

Costa Rica may be a small Central American country, but it contains approximately 500,000 species of animals, birds, and plants. Look online to discover what kinds of animals live there.

Tropical rainforests lie close to the **equator** and are warm, wet regions. Some get 80 inches (203 centimeters) of rain a year, while others get 1 inch (2.5 cm) of rain almost every day. Rainforests are also high in what scientists call **biodiversity**. This means a large number of different plants and animals dwell there.

However, a lot of trees with-in the forest are cut down. This is called **deforestation**, and it happens for many reasons. Loggers cut down

Eighty percent of all insects live in tropical rainforests like the ones in Costa Rica.

MAKE A GUESS!

Where are the world's rainforests? Do some research online to see if your guess was correct!

trees to make wood for industry and construction. Developers clear forests to make room for new homes and businesses. Unfortunately, deforestation leaves many species of animals and plants in danger of becoming **extinct**.

In 1999, two 9-year-old residents of Costa Rica felt their beloved rainforest was disappearing in front of their eyes. Instead of just worrying, the girls decided to act. Kids Saving the Rainforest was their answer to the problems facing them.

Every second, 4,800 square yards (4,013 square meters) of rainforest are destroyed. How much rainforest is destroyed in a minute? An hour?

THINK!

In what kind of climate do you live? Is it warm and rainy like a rainforest? Hot and dry like a desert? Freezing and snowy like an Arctic region?

THE ACCIDENTAL PHILANTHROPISTS

Janine Licare and Aislin Livingstone hadn't set out to fix the world. In fact Janine, who was born in the United States, and Aislin, who's from Canada, simply began as kids wanting to earn spending money. The two friends set up an arts and crafts stand in the middle of their beachside town, Manuel Antonio. They made pretty papier-mâché

Costa Rica is a small country in Central America. It has coastline on both the Atlantic and Pacific Oceans.

ASK QUESTIONS!

Rainforest plants are used to make medicines that help treat everything from malaria to leukemia. What kinds of plants and flowers are used? Search online or at the library to find out how they help.

crafts by hand that drew lots of attention—and sales, too.

There wasn't much for two young girls to spend money on in their small town. The girls decided the money should go for something useful. With $80 from their earnings—and another $80 that Janine's mother, Jennifer Rice, gave them—they bought some land in the rainforest.

They took a road trip to see their land. But when they got there, there

Before they decided to spend their money on land, Janine and Aislin tried out all the fanciest foods in their town.

THINK!

Janine's and Aislin's arts and crafts brought in thousands of dollars a year. What would you do with the money you earned from a successful business? Would you help your family? Would you donate it? Would you put it back into the business to help it grow? Would you buy cool things for yourself?

was no money and no land. A scam! The girls swore to never let that happen to anyone else. They started Kids Saving the Rainforest (KSTR).

They started planting **saplings**. People who donated money to KSTR also adopted a sapling. When it was planted, the girls added wood signs with the names of those who had adopted it. By 2016, they had planted more than 7,000 trees. They are trying to **reforest** 94,000 trees.

Many organizations give gifts to people who donate money. KSTR gives donors trees!

MAKE A GUESS!

Do you know what a rainforest canopy is? Hint: the definition of canopy is "a protective covering."

In 2000, the girls discovered that their favorite titi monkeys were in danger. There were only 1,300 left in the world. Because they were losing their forest, the monkeys would explore the city.

The city's electrical wires and cars were dangerous, though. KSTR started working with electric companies and built "monkey bridges." These ropes that hang above the roads now give monkeys a safe way to cross streets. More than 3,000 titi monkeys now populate the region.

The titi monkey common in Costa Rica is called the Central American squirrel monkey.

ASK QUESTIONS!

We all know Curious George liked the Man in the Yellow Hat because he looked like a banana. Should monkeys eat bananas? Search the Internet and your library to discover why monkeys should not eat bananas. What should they eat?

ONE SPECIES AT A TIME

The original plan for KSTR was to teach kids about the rainforest and empower them to help save it. But KSTR has grown to so much more. Monkey bridges and reforesting were just the beginning.

For the last nine years, KSTR has **rehabilitated** animals at its Wildlife Rescue Center. Wildlife veterinarian Dr. Pia Martin works with a team of

The KSTR Wildlife Rescue Center employs wildlife veterinarians, biologists, vet technicians, and a wildlife manager.

LOOK!

How much oxygen do rainforests produce? Why do we need oxygen? Take a look around online and find out.

other doctors, scientists, and a lot of volunteers. Together they care for about 200 wild animals a year. The goal is to be able to release them back into the wild.

Animals that cannot be released live in the KSTR Wildlife Sanctuary. The team works hard to keep these animals healthy.

Janine, still involved with KSTR, and Aislin are college graduates. The work to help save the rainforest is never finished.

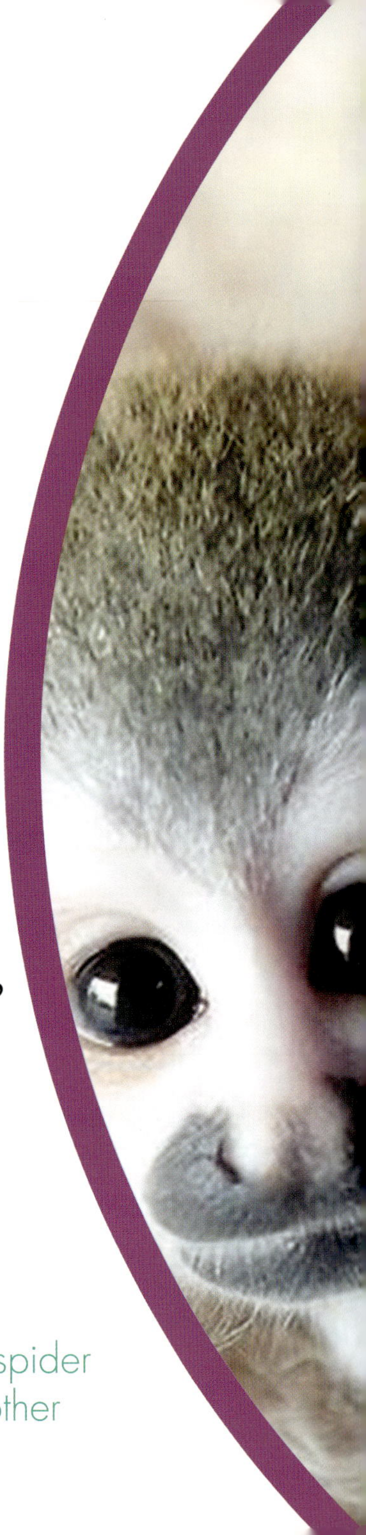

Dr. Martin and KSTR have helped squirrel monkeys, spider monkeys, sloths, kinkajous, jaguarundis, and many other rainforest animals.

CREATE!

Teach others about conservation and Kids Saving the Rainforest by making 10 signs on construction paper that encourage people to recycle and plant trees. Be creative! Put them up around your school.

GLOSSARY

biodiversity (bye-oh-duh-VUR-sih-tee) the condition of nature in which a wide variety of species live in a single area

deforestation (dee-for-is-TAYE-shuhn) cutting down a lot of trees

equator (ih-KWAY-tur) an imaginary line around the middle of the earth that is an equal distance from the North and South Poles

extinct (ik-STINGKT) no longer in existence

photosynthesis (foh-toh-SIN-thi-sis) a chemical process by which green plants and some other organisms make their food

reforest (ree-FOR-ist) to plant new trees on land exposed by cutting or fire

rehabilitated (ree-huh-BIL-ih-tay-ted) restored to a condition of good health

saplings (SAP-lingz) young trees

FIND OUT MORE

WEB SITES

http://kids.nationalgeographic.com/explore/countries/costa-rica/#costa-rica-tree-frog.jpg
National Geographic Kids provides a wonderful overview of Costa Rica.

www.kidssavingtherainforest.org
Learn more about Kids Saving the Rainforest and what it does.

www.mongabay.com
Mongabay is an environmental science and conservation news and information site.

INDEX

ABOUT THE AUTHORS

David Sherman and Melissa Sherman Pearl are cousins who understand and appreciate that you don't have to be an adult to make a difference.